st~~udent~~
DARES

SADIE CAYMAN

summersdale

STUDENT DARES

First published in 2005
Reprinted 2008 and 2010
This edition copyright © Summersdale Publishers Ltd, 2016

Summersdale Publishers Ltd
46 West Street
Chichester
West Sussex
PO19 1RP
UK

www.summersdale.com

Printed and bound in Malta

ISBN: 978-1-84953-945-6

Substantial discounts on bulk quantities of Summersdale books
are available to corporations, professional associations and
other organisations. For details contact Nicky Douglas by tele-
phone: +44 (0) 1243 756902, fax: +44 (0) 1243 786300 or email:
nicky@summersdale.com.

CONTENTS

ABOUT THE AUTHOR

Sadie Cayman attended school, college and university, and left a trail of destruction and confusion in her wake. She is also the author of *Office Dares* and *Naughty Dares*.

INTRODUCTION

This book contains dares to be played in the classroom, the library, in halls of residence and during extracurricular activities. Feel free to mix it up and make things even more interesting!

Remember: we're all in this together. It's up to each and every one of us to rise to the challenge and make learning institutions across the land a little bit more tolerable. It's time to embrace your inner delinquent.

DISCLAIMER

Playing *Student Dares* may not reward you with the grades you've always dreamt of, but rest assured that you'll leave the classroom knowing that you've brightened up the day of every student. Or just confused the hell out of them.

A NOTE ON THE POINTS SYSTEM

The dares have been given a carefully graded point system. Warm yourself up with the 1-point dares: they are perfect for the confident beginner, or your first day in a new group.

The 3-point dares are relatively easy to perform but are often so subtle they may go unnoticed.

The 5-point dares are not to be taken lightly. They're challenging and somewhat outrageous. Expect very puzzled glances and to lose friends.

If your course is coming to an end, by all means turn straight to the 10-point dares. Don't blame me for the consequences.

Play the game, if you dare…

IN THE CLASSROOM

From primary school through to university, the classroom remains the educational and social hub of the academic world. The perfect place to unleash your daring side…

1-POINT DARES

DARE 1

Arrive 20 minutes early for a lesson and stand to attention outside the door. If anyone questions you, simply reply (in character), 'If I told you that I'm afraid I'd have to kill you.'

Rating:

DARE 2

When responding to a question, raise two hands instead of one.

Rating: ⭐

DARE 3

Put your hand up and when asked to speak, say something completely irrelevant like, 'My grandma looks after forty stick insects' or 'My father eats camels'.

Rating:

DARE 4

Keep a fork in your pencil case. When your lecturer asks you to do something, look at them through the prongs and imagine them serving time.

Rating: ⭐

At the end of class, shake your tutor's hand and congratulate them on an excellent lesson.

DARE 5

Rating: ⭐

DARE

See how many times you can get away with going to the toilet during one lesson. Blame it on that suspiciously green chicken you had last night.

Rating: ⭐

Before class, agree with a friend some buzzwords that your teacher is bound to say, e.g. 'ionic bonding' or 'molecule' if it's chemistry. Stand up when you hear the trigger words.

DARE 7

Rating: ⭐

3-POINT DARES

DARE 1

In an English seminar, mutter lines from Shakespearean plays under your breath. If interrupted, reply with a dramatic rendition of Mercutio's death speech: 'A plague on both your houses!'

Rating: ★ ★ ★

DARE 2

When your name is called in a register, say, 'I'll answer to that this time, but in future please refer to me as Hercules.'

Rating: ★ ★ ★

DARE 3

When your tutor mentions
a number, call out, 'Bingo!'
Apologise and explain
that you got confused.

Rating: ★ ★ ★

DARE 4

In the space of ten minutes, answer every single question the teacher asks – even if you don't know the answer.

Rating: ★ ★ ★

Stay behind after class and ask the cleaners if they wouldn't mind giving you a quick vacuum.

DARE 5

Rating: ★ ★ ★

DARE 6

Make a paper banner that reads, *You're a genius* and unroll it at the end of a lecture, as a gesture of appreciation for the guest speaker.

Rating: ★ ★ ★

At the start of a class, place your chair at the tutor's desk and ask for some one-to-one tuition. Remain at the front for the rest of the class, regardless of how your tutor responds.

DARE 7

Rating: ⭐⭐⭐

5-POINT DARES

DARE 1

Leave whatever lesson you're in at 11.30 a.m. on the dot, proclaiming that it's time for a yoga break.

Rating: ★ ★ ★ ★ ★

DARE 2

Stand up and demand
to know the real reason
you're all together
in the classroom.

Rating: ★ ★ ★ ★ ★

DARE 3

Midway through a lesson, pull out a packed lunch and begin eating. If your actions are questioned, ask, 'Don't we get a break?' Offer your teacher a crisp.

Rating: ★★★★★

DARE 4

Refer to your teacher as Chief every time you speak to them.

Rating: ★★★★★

Dispute everything your tutor says – no matter how simple. Ask, 'Can you prove it?'

DARE 5

Rating: ★ ★ ★ ★ ★

DARE 6

Arrive early for a class and rearrange all of the tables into a makeshift fort of which you are king/queen.

Rating: ★ ★ ★ ★ ★

During class,
slowly edge your chair
towards the door. Speed
up every time you are
interrupted or questioned.

DARE 7

Rating: ★ ★ ★ ★ ★

10-POINT DARES

DARE 1

Carve a bust of your tutor out of a potato. Tie a ribbon round it and present it to them at the beginning of the class. Demand extra credit.

Rating: ★★★★★★★★★★

DARE 2

Arrange for a clown to come and perform during a seminar. Audience participation encouraged.

Rating: ★★★★★★★★★★★

DARE 3

During a French class,
stand up and as you
storm out yell,
'This is *not* Russian.'

Rating: ★★★★★★★★★★★

DARE 4

Knock on the staffroom door and ask if anyone is up for a pint after class.

Rating: ★★★★★★★★★★★

Throw a surprise party for your tutor. Insist that you can't start the class until they've had a piece of cake.

DARE **5**

Rating: ★ ★ ★ ★ ★ ★ ★ ★ ★ ★

DARE 6

Instead of taking notes, draw a caricature of your tutor, entitled *Professor Brainy McBrainface*. Leave it on their desk as you leave.

Rating: ★★★★★★★★★★★

Make a sound clip on
your phone of you saying,
'Hello? I'm stuck in here...
I'm frightened... Hello?'
Put the recording on
a loop, and place your
phone inside your bag.

DARE 7

Rating: ★ ★ ★ ★ ★ ★ ★ ★ ★ ★

SCORES

There were a total of **133** points up for grabs in this section.

If you scored **0–50** points: You call yourself daring? You need to raise your game.

You scored **51–100** points: A good effort. Now move onto the library dares: they will really test your skill.

If you scored **101+** points: That's the spirit! Keep up the excellent work.

IN THE LIBRARY

The library. A place of quiet study and calm repose. Or, depending on how you look at it, the Student Dare Land of Opportunity…

1-POINT DARES

DARE 1

Go up to the front desk and ask where you might find the books. A straight face must be maintained for you to win the point.

Rating:

DARE 2

Skip round the library
instead of walking.

Rating: ⭐

DARE 3

Carry a pile of books so huge it completely obscures your view. Award yourself an extra point for each person you bump into.

Rating: ⭐

DARE 4

Pull up a chair next to a stranger, get as close as you can and stare at their open book. When they look at you, say, 'So, what are we reading?'

Rating: ⭐

Settle down to read
a book. Every time
you turn a page,
emit a loud groan.

DARE 5

Rating: ⭐

DARE 6

When checking out books, hand over your supermarket loyalty card. Request reward points.

Rating:

3-POINT DARES

DARE 1

Organise a group of people
to make a low humming
noise while keeping
straight faces. Keep it up
for as long as you can.

Rating: ★ ★ ★

DARE 2

Read out loud, so
everyone can hear,
in a slow voice.
The wordier the
book, the better.

Rating: ★ ★ ★

DARE 3

Eyeball someone through the gap in the shelves. When they move, you move.

Rating: ★ ★ ★

DARE 4

If a member of staff passes with a trolley of books, offer to push it for them. Wheel it in the opposite direction.

Rating: ★ ★ ★

Take your chair into the lift and visit all the floors, until you're asked to leave.

DARE 5

Rating: ★ ★ ★

DARE 6

Move to the quietest
area of the library.
Shush everyone at
regular intervals.

Rating: ★ ★ ★

Try this conversation.
Repeat five times.
Whisper to someone,
'Can you hear that?'
They reply, 'What?'
You say, 'Oh, nothing.'

DARE 7

Rating: ⭐⭐⭐

5-POINT DARES

DARE 1

Ask a member of staff
to help you find a book
you've had trouble locating.
Hold the book in your
hands, in full view.

Rating: ★ ★ ★ ★ ★

DARE 2

Build a tower of books and see how high you can make it. Use a library stepladder or stool to reach when it gets too high to reach from the floor.

Rating: ★ ★ ★ ★ ★

DARE 3

Walk around the library slowly
and try to push the bookshelves.
Pull on books as if they're levers.
Tell people you're looking
for the secret passageway.

Rating: ★ ★ ★ ★ ★

DARE 4

Set off the security
sensors at the door
and drop to the floor,
crying, 'I knew you'd
find me eventually.'

Rating: ★ ★ ★ ★ ★

Approach the student who seems most engrossed in their book. Say, 'I'm afraid I'm going to have to ask you to leave.' If they ask why, simply reply, 'You know the rules.'

DARE 5

Rating: ★★★★★

10-POINT DARES

DARE 1

Take all the books off the bottom shelf of a secluded area. Climb on to the shelf and lie down; stay perfectly still. Wait for someone to browse nearby, then yawn, slowly roll out from your makeshift napping space, stand up and walk away.

Rating: ★★★★★★★★★★★

DARE 2

Move around the library as if you're on a top secret mission. Creep along the walls, army crawl across the floor... Humming the *Mission Impossible* theme tune is optional.

Rating: ★★★★★★★★★★★

DARE 3

Run a lap of the library at high speed. Look at your watch and announce a personal best. Repeat until physically restrained.

Rating: ★★★★★★★★★★★

SCORES

There were a total of **83** points up for grabs in this section.

If you scored **0–20** points: Are you even trying?

If you scored **21–50** points: You're really getting the hang of this now – and you're starting to love it, aren't you?

If you scored **51+** points: Excellent work. Have you noticed your tutor's worry lines getting deeper?

IN THE HALLS OF RESIDENCE

University halls of residence are often the first place we get to live away from home. The following dares provide the perfect opportunity to make friends or enemies for life...

1-POINT DARES

DARE 1

Unpack your belongings in someone else's bedroom and ask them, 'Where's the best place to put my ant collection?'

Rating: ⭐

DARE 2

Ignore the first five people who say hello to you. Enthusiastically hug the sixth.

Rating:

DARE 3

Leave your underwear
hanging in the shower.

Rating: ⭐

DARE 4

Create a fake spider out of pipe cleaners. Hide it behind the butter in the fridge.

Rating:

Walk up to people and
ask them, very seriously,
'Do you know the
muffin man?'

DARE **5**

Rating: ⭐

DARE 6

Announce when you're going to the bathroom. Be sure to specify which number it will be.

Rating:

Cooking a meal for your hall-mates is a perfect way to make friends. Prepare turnip soup for the starter, a liver stew for the main course, and for dessert – a trifle made with fish.

DARE 7

Rating: ⭐

3-POINT DARES

DARE 1

Go into the room of a hall-mate the night before an important deadline and, while they watch you with growing irritation, turn the light switch on and off ten times.

Rating: ★ ★ ★

DARE 2

Ask your hall-mates mysterious questions then scribble furiously in a notebook. Mutter something about 'psychological profiles'.

Rating: ★ ★ ★

DARE 3

Hide all of the pots and pans in the kitchen. For an extra point, turn it into a treasure hunt.

Rating: ★ ★ ★

DARE 4

Buy a leek and put
it on top of the
toilet. Tell everybody
that there's a leak
in the bathroom.

Rating: ★ ★ ★

Keep a picture of David Hasselhoff with you at all times. Show it to everyone you meet, and tell them that he is your grandfather.

DARE 5

Rating: ★ ★ ★

DARE 6

Five days in advance,
tell your friends you
can't attend their
party because you're
not in the mood.

Rating: ★ ★ ★

Put a huge bowl of jelly right outside someone's door. Fill the same person's shoes with more jelly, just in case they missed it the first time.

DARE 7

Rating: ★ ★ ★

5-POINT DARES

DARE 1

Stick *Do not touch* labels on all of your possessions that are kept in communal areas – even on those speakers you said everyone could use.

Rating: ★★★★★

DARE 2

Flirt with your room-mate's partner really badly. Lick your lips when they talk to you and wink at them when they leave.

Rating: ★ ★ ★ ★ ★

DARE 3

Bake a chocolate cake for everyone and lace it with chilli powder. Enjoy watching them pretend it's delicious.

Rating: ★ ★ ★ ★ ★

DARE 4

Late at night accuse someone of eating your cheese. Burst into sobs and say you're moving out. In the morning, say you don't remember any of this.

Rating: ★★★★★

Perform a morning ritual of 'underwear yoga' in a communal room, while playing loud yet soothing rainforest sounds.

DARE 5

Rating: ★ ★ ★ ★ ★

DARE 6

Fashion a holster belt for the remote control and wear it with pride. Growl if anybody else asks to use the remote.

Rating:

Spend a day accusing
everyone you meet of being
a spy. The following day,
deny all knowledge of this.

DARE 7

Rating: ★★★★★

10-POINT DARES

DARE 1

Choose one bartender at the union/a student bar and tell them you're thinking of quitting your course to become an astronaut. Repeat every night for a week, choosing a different career each time.

Rating: ★★★★★★★★★★★★

DARE 2

Knock on the hall warden's door at 3 a.m. and invite yourself in for a nightcap.

Rating: ★ ★ ★ ★ ★ ★ ★ ★ ★ ★

DARE 3

Stand beneath someone's window and perform the Chesney Hawkes classic 'The One and Only'.

Rating: ★ ★ ★ ★ ★ ★ ★ ★ ★ ★

SCORES

There were a total of **94** points up for grabs in this section.

If you scored **0–40** points: You're a loser. Give this book to someone with balls.

If you scored **41–80** points: Good work. Give yourself a pat on the back.

If you scored **81+** points: You're a shining example of daring behaviour. Bravo!

EXTRA-CURRICULAR ACTIVITIES

Whether you're captain of the football team or a member of the chess club, there's a ludicrous dare for you to undertake in this section.

1-POINT DARES

DARE 1

Join the chess club and
bring a snakes and ladders
board to the first session.

Rating:

DARE 2

Turn up to trampoline club wearing a crash helmet.

Rating:

DARE 3

Go to swimming club
wearing armbands.
If asked to remove them,
sob like a baby and ask
for your mummy.

Rating:

DARE 4

Arrive at the football try-outs in full rugby kit. Tackle your teammates rugby-style.

Rating:

Join the film society.
At the first meeting
ask when *Bambi* will
be screened.

DARE 5

Rating:

DARE 6

Attend badminton training. Whenever the coach says the word 'shuttlecock', have a hysterical giggling fit.

Rating:

3-POINT DARES

DARE 1

Join the volleyball team. Call your teammates 'Champ' and 'Tiger', and encourage them to refer to you as 'Coach'. Initiate high fives at every opportunity.

Rating: ★ ★ ★

DARE 2

When auditioning for the choir, perform a thrash metal song... badly.

Rating: ★★★

DARE 3

Attend a meeting of the literature appreciation society. Compare and contrast the characters of Spider-Man and Batman. Claim Spider-Man is a latter-day Hamlet and Batman is Macbeth.

Rating: ★ ★ ★

DARE 4

While playing football/netball, at a random point in the game run off the pitch screaming and waving your arms in the air.

Rating: ★ ★ ★

Turn up to a cricket practice wearing a ballgown, or bow tie and tails.

DARE 5

Rating: ★ ★ ★

DARE 6

Go to an art class
and create a life-size
papier mâché model
of yourself – naked.

Rating: ★ ★ ★

5-POINT DARES

DARE **1**

Attend a dance class. Put on 'Gangnam Style' and perform the dance. Award yourself an extra point if you sing along at the same time.

Rating: ★ ★ ★ ★ ★

DARE 2

Audition for the orchestra... on the kazoo.

Rating: ★ ★ ★ ★ ★

DARE 3

After training, kneel in front of the water fountain and exclaim, 'Have you *tried* this stuff? It's so refreshing!' Then insist that everyone drinks some.

Rating: ★ ★ ★ ★ ★

DARE 4

At the end of a football/
netball/hockey match, say
that it would be nice if
you concluded by singing
the national anthem.
Award yourself an extra
point for starting it off.

Rating: ★★★★★

During athletics training, hop on one leg in every exercise.

DARE 5

Rating: ★★★★★

DARE 6

Become a member of the amateur dramatics society. Cultivate a new accent for your stage persona, e.g. German, Scottish or Transylvanian. As soon as you leave the stage, revert to your own accent.

Rating: ★ ★ ★ ★ ★

10-POINT DARES

DARE 1

Turn up at gymnastics club and immediately begin doing forward rolls across the floor. If questioned, complain that they've interrupted your Olympic routine.

Rating: ★★★★★★★★★★

DARE 2

At the swimming pool, bellyflop as loudly as possible into the water and doggy-paddle into other swimmers' lanes. Ask if you've made the team.

Rating: ★★★★★★★★★★

DARE 3

During athletics training, squat in the sandpit and pretend to take a number two.

Rating: ★★★★★★★★★★